Light on the Path
and Karma

WRITTEN DOWN BY

M. C.

WITH NOTES AND COMMENTS

LONDON
THEOSOPHICAL PUBLISHING HOUSE
9 ST MARTIN'S STREET, W.C. 2

Reprinted 1920

LIGHT ON THE PATH

I

THESE rules are written for all disciples:
Attend you to them.

Before the eyes can see they must be
incapable of tears. Before the ear can
hear it must have lost its sensitiveness.
Before the voice can speak in the presence
of the Masters it must have lost the power
to wound. Before the soul can stand in
the presence of the Masters its feet must
be washed in the blood of the heart.

  1. Kill out ambition.[1]

---

[1] Ambition is the first curse: the great tempter
of the man who is rising above his fellows.
It is the simplest form of looking for reward.
Men of intelligence and power are led away from
their higher possibilities by it continually. Yet
it is a necessary teacher. Its results turn to
dust and ashes in the mouth; like death and

estrangement it shows the man at last that to work for self is to work for disappointment. But though this first rule seems so simple and easy, do not quickly pass it by. For these vices of the ordinary man pass through a subtle transformation and reappear with changed aspect in the heart of the disciple. It is easy to say: "I will not be ambitious"; it is not so easy to say: "When the Master reads my heart, He will find it clean utterly." The pure artist who works for the love of his work is sometimes more firmly planted on the right road than the Occultist who fancies he has removed his interest from self, but who has in reality only enlarged the limits of experience and desire, and transferred his interest to the things which concern his larger span of life. The same principle applies to the other two seemingly simple rules. Linger over them, and do not let yourself be easily deceived by your own heart. For now, at the threshold, a mistake can be corrected. But carry it on with you and it will grow and come to fruition, or else you must suffer bitterly in its destruction.

2. Kill out desire of life.

3. Kill out desire of comfort.

4. Work as those work who are ambitious. Respect life as those do who desire it. Be happy as those are who live for happiness.

Seek in the heart the source of evil and expunge it. It lives fruitfully in the heart of the devoted disciple as well as in the heart of the man of desire. Only the strong can kill it out. The weak must wait for its growth, its fruition, its death. And it is a plant that lives and increases throughout the ages. It flowers when the man has accumulated unto himself innumerable existences. He who will enter upon the path of power must tear this thing out of his heart. And then the heart will bleed, and the whole life of the man seem to be utterly dissolved. This ordeal must be endured: it may come at the first step of the perilous ladder which leads to the path of life: it may not come until the last. But, O disciple, remember that it has to be endured, and fasten the energies of your soul upon the task. Live neither in the present nor the future, but in the Eternal. This giant weed cannot flower there: this blot upon existence is wiped out by the very atmosphere of eternal thought.

5. Kill out all sense of separateness.[2]

[2] Do not fancy you can stand aside from the bad man or the foolish man. They are yourself, though in a less degree than your friend or your Master. But if you allow the idea of separateness from any evil thing or person to grow up within you, by so doing you create karma, which will bind you to that thing or person till your soul recognizes that it cannot be isolated. Remember that the sin and shame of the world are your sin and shame; for you are a part of it; your karma is inextricably interwoven with the great Karma. And before you can attain knowledge you must have passed through all places, foul and clean alike. Therefore, remember that the soiled garment you shrink from touching may have been yours yesterday, may be yours to-morrow. And if you turn with horror from it, when it is flung upon your shoulders, it will cling the more closely to you. The self-righteous man makes for himself a bed of mire. Abstain because it is right to abstain, not that yourself shall be kept clean.

6. Kill out desire for sensation.

7. Kill out the hunger for growth.

8. Yet stand alone and isolated, because nothing that is embodied, nothing that is conscious of separation, nothing that is out of the Eternal, can aid you. Learn from sensation · and observe it, because only so can you commence the science of self-knowledge, and plant your foot on the first step of the ladder. Grow as the flower grows, unconsciously, but eagerly anxious to open its soul to the air. So must you press forward to open your soul to the Eternal. But it must be the Eternal that draws forth your strength and beauty, not desire of growth. For in the one case you develop in the luxuriance of purity; in the other you harden by the forcible passion for personal stature.

9. Desire only that which is within you.

10. Desire only that which is beyond you.

11. Desire only that which is unattainable.

12. For within you is the light .of the

world—the only light that can be shed upon the path. If you are unable to perceive it within you, it is useless to look for it elsewhere. It is beyond you, because when you reach it you have lost yourself. It is unattainable, because it for ever recedes. You will enter the light, but you will never touch the Flame.

13. Desire power ardently.

14. Desire peace fervently.

15. Desire possessions above all.

16. But those possessions must belong to the pure soul only, and be possessed therefore by all pure souls equally, and thus be the especial property of the whole only when united. Hunger for such possessions as can be held by the pure soul, that you may accumulate wealth for that united spirit of life which is your only true self. The peace you shall desire is that sacred peace which nothing can disturb, and in which the soul grows as does the holy flower upon the still lagoons.

And that power which the disciple shall covet is that which shall make him appear as nothing in the eyes of men.

17. Seek out the way.[3]

[3] These four words seem, perhaps, too slight to stand alone. The disciple may say, "Should I study these thoughts at all did I not seek out the way?" Yet do not pass on hastily. Pause and consider awhile. Is it the way you desire, or is it that there is a dim perspective in your visions of great heights to be scaled by yourself, of a great future for you to compass? Be warned. The way is to be sought for its own sake, not with regard to your feet that shall tread it.

There is a correspondence between this rule and the seventeenth of the second series. When after ages of struggle and many victories the final battle is won, the final secret demanded, then you are prepared for a further path. When the final secret of this great lesson is told, in it is opened the mystery of the new way—a path which leads out of all human experience, and which is utterly beyond human perception or imagination. At each of these points it is needful to pause long and consider well. At each of these points it is necessary to be sure that the way is chosen for its own sake. The way and the truth come first, then follows the life.

18. Seek the way by retreating within.

19. Seek the way by advancing boldly without.

20. Seek it not by any one road. To each temperament there is one road which seems the most desirable. But the way is not found by devotion alone, by religious contemplation alone, by ardent progress, by self-sacrificing labour, by studious observation of life. None alone can take the disciple more than one step onward. All steps are necessary to make up the ladder. The vices of men become steps in the ladder, one by one, as they are surmounted. The virtues of men are steps indeed, necessary—not by any means to be dispensed with. Yet, though they create a fair atmosphere and a happy future, they are useless if they stand alone. The whole nature of man must be used wisely by the one who desires to enter the way. Each man is to himself absolutely the way, the truth, and the life.

But he is only so when he grasps his whole individuality firmly, and by the force of his awakened spiritual will recognizes this individuality as not himself, but that thing which he has with pain created for his own use and by means of which he purposes, as his growth slowly develops his intelligence, to reach to the life beyond individuality. When he knows that for this his wonderful complex, separated life exists, then indeed, and then only, he is upon the way. Seek it by plunging into the mysterious and glorious depths of your own inmost being. Seek it by testing all experience, by utilizing the senses in order to understand the growth and meaning of individuality, and the beauty and obscurity of those other divine fragments which are struggling side by side with you, and form the race to which you belong. Seek it by study of the laws of being, the laws of nature, the laws of the supernatural; and seek it by making the profound obeisance of the soul to the dim star that burns within. Steadily, as you watch and worship, its light will grow stronger. Then you may know you have found the beginning of the way. And when you have found the end, its light will suddenly become the infinite light.[4]

[4] Seek it by testing all experience; and remember that when I say this I do not say: "Yield to the seductions of sense in order to know it." Before you have become an Occultist you may do this; but not afterwards. When you have chosen and entered the Path you cannot yield to these seductions without shame. Yet you can experience them without horror: can weigh, observe and test them, and wait with the patience of confidence for the hour when they shall affect you no longer.* But do not condemn the man that yields; stretch out your hand to him as a brother pilgrim whose feet have become heavy with mire. Remember, O disciple, that great though the gulf may be between the good

---

* [*That is, if these seductions are felt, they should be calmly analyzed, impersonally judged, that the lesson conveyed by them may be learned. But to yield to them is shame.—Ed.*]

man and the sinner, it is greater between the good man and the man who has attained knowledge; it is immeasurable between the good man and the one on the threshold of divinity. Therefore be wary lest too soon you fancy yourself a thing apart from the mass. When you have found the beginning of the way the star of your soul will show its light; and by that light you will perceive how great is the darkness in which it burns. Mind, heart, brain, all are obscure and dark until the first great battle has been won. Be not appalled and terrified by the sight; keep your eyes fixed on the small light and it will grow. But let the darkness within help you to understand the helplessness of those who have seen no light, whose souls are in profound gloom. Blame them not. Shrink not from them, but try to lift a little of the heavy karma of the world; give your aid to the few strong hands that hold back the powers of darkness from obtaining complete victory. Then do you enter into a partnership of joy, which brings indeed terrible toil and profound sadness, but also a great and ever-increasing delight.

21. Look for the flower to bloom in the silence that follows the storm: not till then.

It shall grow, it will shoot up, it will make branches and leaves and form buds, while the storm continues, while the battle lasts.   But not till the whole personality of the man is dissolved and melted—not until it is held by the divine fragment which has created it, as a mere subject for grave experiment and experience—not until the whole nature has yielded and become subject unto its Higher Self, can the bloom open.   Then will come a calm such as comes in a tropical country after the heavy rain, when Nature works so swiftly that one may see her action.   Such a calm will come to the harassed spirit. And in the deep silence the mysterious event will occur which will prove that the way has been found.   Call it by what name you will, it is a voice that speaks where there is none to speak—it is a messenger that comes, a messenger without form or substance; or it is the flower of the soul that has opened.   It cannot be described by any metaphor.   But it can be felt after, looked for, and desired, even amid the raging of the storm. The silence may last a moment of time or it may last a thousand years. But it will end. Yet you will carry its strength with you. Again and again the battle must be fought and won. It is only for an interval that Nature can be still.[5]

[5] The opening of the bloom is the glorious moment when perception awakes: with it come confidence, knowledge, certainty. The pause of the soul is the moment of wonder, and the next moment of satisfaction, that is the silence.

Know, O disciple, that those who have passed through the silence, and felt its peace and retained its strength, they long that you shall pass through it also. Therefore, in the Hall of Learning, when he is capable of entering there, the disciple will always find his Master.

Those that ask shall have. But though the ordinary man asks perpetually, his voice is not heard. For he asks with his mind only; and the voice of the mind is only heard on that plane on which the mind acts. Therefore, not until the first twenty-one rules are passed do I say those that ask shall have.

To read, in the occult sense, is to read with the eyes of the spirit. To ask is to feel the hunger within—the yearning of spiritual aspiration. To be able to read means having obtained the power in a small degree of gratifying that hunger. When the disciple is ready to learn, then he is accepted, acknowledged, recognized. It must be so, for he has lit his lamp, and it cannot be hidden. But to learn is impossible until the first great battle has been won. The mind may recognize truth, but the spirit cannot receive it. Once having passed through the storm and attained the peace, it is then always possible to learn, even though the disciple waver, hesitate, and turn aside. The Voice of the Silence remains within him, and though he leave the Path utterly, yet one day it will resound, and rend him asunder and separate his passions from his divine possibilities. Then, with pain and desperate cries from the deserted lower self, he will return.

Therefore I say, Peace be with you, "My peace I give unto you," can only be said by the Master to the beloved disciples who are as himself. There are some even among those who are ignorant of the Eastern wisdom, to whom this can be said, and to whom it can daily be said with more completeness.

△ Regard the three truths. They are equal.

These written above are the first of the rules which are written on the walls of the Hall of Learning. Those that ask

shall have.   Those that desire to read
shall read.   Those that desire to learn
shall learn.

PEACE BE WITH YOU.

△

II

Out of the silence that is peace a resonant voice shall arise. And this voice will say: It is not well; thou hast reaped, now thou must sow. And knowing this voice to be the silence itself thou wilt obey.

Thou who art now a disciple, able to stand, able to hear, able to see, able to speak; who hast conquered desire and attained to self-knowledge; who hast seen thy soul in its bloom and recognized it, and heard the Voice of the Silence—go thou to the Hall of Learning and read what is written there for thee.[6]

[6] To be able to stand is to have confidence; to be able to hear is to have opened the doors of the soul: to be able to see is to have attained perception; to be able to speak is to have

attained the power of helping others; to have conquered desire is to have learned how to use and control the self; to have attained to self-knowledge is to have retreated to the inner fortress whence the personal man can be viewed with impartiality; to have seen the soul in its bloom is to have obtained a momentary glimpse in thyself of the transfiguration which shall eventually make thee more than man; to recognize is to achieve the great task of gazing upon the blazing light without dropping the eyes and not falling back in terror, as though before some ghastly phantom. This happens to some, and so when the victory is all but won it is lost. To hear the Voice of the Silence is to understand that from within comes the only true guidance: to go to the Hall of Learning is to enter the state in which learning becomes possible. Then will many words be written there for thee, and written in fiery letters for thee easily to read. For when the disciple is ready, the Master is ready also.

1. Stand aside in the coming battle, and though thou fightest be not thou the warrior.

2. Look for the Warrior, and let him fight in thee.

3. Take his orders for battle, and obey them.

4. Obey him, not as though he were a general, but as though he were thyself, and his spoken words were the utterance of thy secret desires; for he is thyself, yet infinitely wiser and stronger than thyself. Look for him, else in the fever and hurry of the fight thou mayest pass him; and he will not know thee unless thou knowest him. If thy cry meet his listening ear, then will he fight in thee, and fill the dull void within. And if this is so, then canst thou go through the fight cool and unwearied, standing aside and letting him battle for thee. Then it will be impossible for thee to strike one blow amiss But if thou look not for him, if thou pass him by, then there is no safeguard for thee. Thy brain will reel, thy heart grow uncertain, and in the dust of the battlefield thy sight and senses will fail, and thou wilt not know thy friends from thy enemies.

He is thyself. Yet thou art but finite and liable to error; he is eternal and is sure. He is eternal truth. When once he has entered thee and become thy Warrior, he will never utterly desert thee; and at the day of the great peace he will become one with thee.

5. Listen to the song of life.[7]

[7] Look for it, and listen to it, first in your own heart. At first you may say, "It is not there; when I search I find only discord." Look deeper. If again you are disappointed, pause and look deeper again. There is a natural melody, an obscure fount in every human heart. It may be hidden over and utterly concealed and silenced—but it is there. At the very base of your nature you will find faith, hope, and love. He that chooses evil refuses to look within himself, shuts his ears to the melody of his heart, as he blinds his eyes to the light of his soul. He does this because he finds it easier to live in desires. But underneath all life is the strong current that cannot be checked; the great waters are there in reality. Find them, and you will perceive that none, not the most wretched of creatures, but is a part of it, however he blind himself to the fact and build up for himself a phantasmal outer form of horror. In that sense it is that I say to you: All those beings among whom you struggle on are fragments of the Divine. And so deceptive is

the illusion in which you live, that it is hard to guess where you will first detect the sweet voice in the hearts of others. But know that it is certainly within yourself. Look for it there, and once having heard it, you will more readily recognize it around you.

6. Store in your memory the melody you hear.

7. Learn from it the lesson of harmony.

8. You can stand upright now, firm as a rock amid the turmoil, obeying the Warrior who is thyself and thy king. Unconcerned in the battle save to do his bidding, having no longer any care as to the result of the battle; for one thing only is important, that the warrior shall win, and you know he is incapable of defeat; standing thus, cool and awakened, use the hearing you have acquired by pain and by the destruction of pain. Only fragments of the great song come to your ears while yet you are but man. But if you listen to it, remember it faithfully, so that none which has reached you is lost,

and endeavour to learn from it the meaning of the mystery which surrounds you
In time you will need no teacher. For
as the individual has voice, so has that
in which the individual exists. Life itself
has speech and is never silent. And its
utterance is not, as you that are deaf may
suppose, a cry: it is a song. Learn from
it that you are part of the harmony; learn
from it to obey the laws of the harmony.

9. Regard earnestly all the life that
surrounds you.

10. Learn to look intelligently into the
hearts of men.[8]

[8] From an absolutely impersonal point of
view, otherwise your sight is coloured. Therefore impersonality must first be understood.

Intelligence is impartial: no man is your
enemy: no man is your friend. All alike are
your teachers. Your enemy becomes a mystery
that must be solved, even though it take ages;
for man must be understood. Your friend
becomes a part of yourself, an extension of yourself, a riddle hard to read. Only one thing is
more difficult to know—your own heart. Not
until the bonds of personality are loosed can

that profound mystery of self begin to be seen. Not till you stand aside from it, will it in any way reveal itself to your understanding. Then, and not till then, can you grasp and guide it. Then, and not till then, can you use all its powers, and devote them to a worthy service.

11. Regard most earnestly your own heart.

12. For through your own heart comes the one light which can illuminate life and make it clear to your eyes.

Study the hearts of men that you may know what is that world in which you live and of which you will to be a part. Regard the constantly changing moving life which surrounds you, for it is formed by the hearts of men; and as you learn to understand their constitution and meaning, you will by degrees be able to read the larger word of life.

13. Speech comes only with knowledge. Attain to knowledge and you will attain to speech.[9]

[9] It is impossible to help others till you have

obtained some certainty of your own. When you have learned the first twenty-one rules and have entered the Hall of Learning, with your powers developed and sense unchained, then you will find there is a fount within you from which speech will arise.

After the thirteenth rule I can add no words to what is already written.

My peace I give unto you. △

These notes are written only for those to whom I give my peace; those who can read what I have written with the inner as well as the outer sense.

14. Having obtained the use of the inner senses, having conquered the desires of the outer senses, having conquered the desires of the individual soul, and having obtained knowledge, prepare now, O disciple, to enter upon the way in reality. The path is found: make yourself ready to tread it.

15. Inquire of the earth, the air, and the water, of the secrets they hold for you. The development of your inner senses will enable you to do this.

16. Inquire of the Holy Ones of the

earth of the secrets they hold for you. The conquering of the desires of the outer senses will give you the right to do this.

17. Inquire of the inmost, the One, of its final secret which it holds for you through the ages.

The great and difficult victory, the conquering of the desires of the individual soul, is a work of ages; therefore expect not to obtain its rewards until ages of experience have been accumulated. When the time of learning this seventeenth rule is reached, man is on the threshold of becoming more than man.

18. The knowledge which is now yours is only yours because your soul has become one with all pure souls and with the inmost. It is a trust vested in you by the Most High. Betray it, misuse your knowledge or neglect it, and it is possible even now for you to fall from the high estate you have attained. Great ones fall

back, even from the threshold, unable to sustain the weight of their responsibility, unable to pass on. Therefore look forward always with awe and trembling to this moment, and be prepared for the battle.

19. It is written that for him who is on the threshold of divinity no law can be framed, no guide can exist. Yet to enlighten the disciple, the final struggle may be thus expressed:

Hold fast to that which has neither substance nor existence.

20. Listen only to the voice which is soundless.

21. Look only on that which is invisible alike to the inner and the outer sense.

PEACE BE WITH YOU

△

COMMENTS

I

BEFORE THE EYES CAN SEE THEY MUST BE INCAPABLE OF TEARS

IT should be very clearly remembered by all readers of this volume that it is a book which may appear to have some little philosophy in it, but very little sense, to those who believe it to be written in ordinary English. To the many who read in this manner it will be—not *caviare* so much as olives strong of their salt. Be warned and read but a little in this way.

There is another way of reading, which is, indeed, the only one of any use with many authors. It is reading not between the lines, but within the words. In fact, it is deciphering a profound cipher. All

alchemical works are written in the cipher
of which I speak; it has been used by the
great philosophers and poets of all time.
It is used systematically by the Adepts in
life and knowledge, who, seemingly giving
out their deepest wisdom, hide in the very
words which frame it its actual mystery.
They cannot do more. There is a law of
Nature which insists that a man shall read
these mysteries for himself. By no other
method can he obtain them. A man who
desires to live must eat his food himself;
this is the simple law of nature—which
applies also to the higher life. A man
who would live and act in it cannot be
fed like a babe with a spoon; he must eat
for himself.

I propose to put into new and sometimes plainer language parts of LIGHT ON
THE PATH; but whether this effort of mine
will really be any interpretation I cannot
say. To a deaf and dumb man a truth is
made no more intelligible if, in order to

make it so, some misguided linguist translate the words in which it is couched into
every living or dead language, and shouts
these different phrases in his ear. But
for those who are not deaf and dumb one
language is generally easier than the rest;
and it is to such as these I address myself.

The very first aphorisms of LIGHT ON
THE PATH, included under Part I, have,
I know well, remained sealed as to their
inner meaning to many who have otherwise followed the purpose of the book.

There are four proven and certain truths
with regard to the entrance to occultism.
The Gates of Gold bar that threshold;
yet there are some who pass those Gates
and discover the sublime and illimitable
beyond. In the far spaces of Time all
will pass those gates. But I am one who
wish that Time, the great deluder, were
not so over-masterful. To those who
know and love him I have no word to
say; but to the others—and there are not

so very few as some may fancy—to whom the passage of time is as the stroke of a sledge-hammer, and the sense of space like the bars of an iron cage, I will translate and re-translate, until they understand fully.

The four truths written on the first page of LIGHT ON THE PATH refer to the trial initiation of the would-be Occultist. Until he has passed it, he cannot even reach to the latch of the Gate which admits to knowledge. Knowledge is man's greatest inheritance; why, then, should he not attempt to reach it by every possible road? The laboratory is not the only ground for experiment; *science*, we must remember, is derived from *sciens*, present participle of *scire*, "to know"; its origin is similar to that of the word "discern," "to ken." Science does not therefore deal only with matter, no, not even its subtlest and obscurest forms. Such an idea is born merely of the idle spirit of the age. Science is a word which covers all forms of knowledge. It is exceedingly interesting to hear what chemists discover, and to see them finding their way through the densities of matter to its finer forms; but there are other kinds of knowledge than this, and it is not everyone who restricts his (strictly scientific) desire for knowledge to experiments which are capable of being tested by the physical senses.

Everyone who is not a dullard, or a man stupefied by some predominant vice, has guessed, or even perhaps discovered with some certainty, that there are subtle senses lying within the physical senses; there is nothing at all extraordinary in this; if we took the trouble to call Nature into the witness-box we should find that everything which is perceptible to the ordinary sight has something even more important than itself hidden within it; the microscope has opened a world to us, but

within those encasements which the microscope reveals, lies a mystery which no
machinery can probe.

The whole world is animated and lit,
down to its most material shapes, by a
world within it. This inner world is called
Astral by some people, and it is as good
a word as any other, though it merely
means starry; but the stars, as Locke
pointed out, are luminous bodies which
give light of themselves. This quality
is characteristic of the light which lies
within matter; for those who see it need
no lamp to see it by. The word " star,"
moreover, is derived from the Anglo-Saxon
" stir-an," to steer, to stir, to move, and
undeniably it is the inner life which is
master of the outer, just as a man's brain
guides the movements of his lips. So that
although Astral is no very excellent word
in itself, I am content to use it for my
present purpose.

The whole of LIGHT ON THE PATH is

written in an astral cipher and can therefore only be deciphered by one who reads astrally. And its teaching is chiefly directed towards the cultivation and development of the astral life. Until the first step has been taken in this development the swift knowledge which is called intuition with certainty, is impossible to man. And this positive and certain intuition is the only form of knowledge which enables a man to work rapidly or reach his true and high estate, within the limit of his conscious effort. To obtain knowledge by experiment is too tedious a method for those who desire to accomplish real work; he who gets it by certain intuition lays hands on its various forms with supreme rapidity, by fierce effort of will; as a determined workman grasps his tools, indifferent to their weight or any other difficulty which may stand in his way. He does not stay for each to be tested—he uses such as he sees are fittest.

All the rules contained in LIGHT ON THE PATH are written for all disciples, but only for disciples—those who "take knowledge." To none else but the student in this school are its laws of any use or interest.

To all who are interested seriously in Occultism, I say first—take knowledge. To him who hath shall be given. It is useless to wait for it. The womb of Time will close before you, and in later years you will remain unborn, without power. I therefore say to those who have any hunger or thirst for knowledge, attend to these Rules.

They are none of my handicraft or invention. They are merely the phrasing of laws in super-nature, the putting into words truths as absolute in their own sphere as those laws which govern the conduct of the earth and its atmosphere.

The senses spoken of in these four statements are the astral, or inner senses.

No man desires to see that light which illumines the spaceless soul until pain and sorrow and despair have driven him away from the life of ordinary humanity. First he wears out pleasure, then he wears out pain—till, at last, his eyes become incapable of tears.

This is a truism, although I know perfectly well that it will meet with a vehement denial from many who are in sympathy with thoughts which spring from the inner life. *To see* with the astral sense of sight is a form of activity which it is difficult for us to understand immediately. The scientist knows very well what a miracle is achieved by each child that is born into the world, when it first conquers its eyesight and compels it to obey its brain. An equal miracle is performed with each sense certainly, but this ordering of sight is perhaps the most stupendous effort. Yet the child does it almost unconsciously, by force of the powerful heredity of habit. No one now is aware that he has ever done it at all; just as we cannot recollect the individual movements which enabled us to walk up a hill a year ago. This arises from the fact that we move and live and have our being in matter. Our knowledge of it has become intuitive.

With our astral life it is very much otherwise. For long years past, man has paid very little attention to it—so little that he has practically lost the use of his senses. It is true, in every civilization the star arises and man confesses, with more or less of folly and confusion, that he knows himself to be. But most often he denies it, and in being a materialist becomes that strange being, a being which cannot see its own light, a thing of life which will not live, an astral animal which has eyes, and ears, and speech, and power, yet will use none of these gifts. This is the case, and the habit of ignorance has become so confirmed, that now none will see with the inner vision till agony has made the physical eyes not only unseeing, but without tears—the moisture of life. To be incapable of tears is to have faced and conquered the simple human nature, and to have attained an equilibrium which cannot be shaken by personal emotions. It does not imply any hardness of heart, or any indifference. It does not imply the exhaustion of sorrow, when the suffering soul seems powerless to suffer acutely any longer; it does not mean the deadness of old age, when emotion is becoming dull because the strings which vibrate to it are wearing out. None of these conditions are fit for a disciple, and if any one of them exist in him, it must be overcome before the Path can be entered upon. Hardness of heart belongs to the selfish man, the egotist, to whom the Gate is for ever closed. Indifference belongs to the fool and the false philosopher; those whose lukewarmness makes them mere puppets, not strong enough to face the realities of existence. When pain or sorrow has worn out the keenness of suffering, the result is a lethargy not unlike that which accompanies old age, as it is usually experienced by men and women. Such a condition makes the entrance to the Path impossible, because the first step is one of difficulty and needs a strong man full of psychic and physical vigour to attempt it.

It is a truth that, as Edgar Allan Poe said, the eyes are the windows for the soul, the windows of that haunted palace in which it dwells. This is the very nearest interpretation into ordinary language of the meaning of the text. If grief, dismay, disappointment or pleasure can shake the soul so that it loses its fixed hold on the calm spirit which inspires it, and the moisture of life breaks forth, drowning knowledge in sensation, then all is blurred, the windows are darkened, the light is useless. This is as literal a fact as that if a man, at the edge of a precipice, loses his nerve through some sudden emotion he will certainly fall. The poise of the body, the balance, must be preserved, not only in dangerous places, but even on level ground, and with all the assistance Nature gives us by the law of gravitation. So it is with the soul: it is the link between the outer body and the starry spirit beyond; the divine spark dwells in the still place where no convulsion of Nature can shake the air; this is so always. But the soul may lose its hold on that, its knowledge of it, even though these two are part of one whole ; and it is by emotion, by sensation, that this hold is loosed. To suffer either pleasure or pain causes a vivid vibration which is, to the consciousness of man, life. Now this sensibility does not lessen when the disciple enters upon his training; it increases. It is the first test of his strength; he must suffer, must enjoy or endure, more keenly than other men, while yet he has taken on him a duty which does not exist for other men, that of not allowing his suffering to shake him from his fixed purpose. He has, in fact, at the first step to take himself steadily in hand and put the bit into his own mouth; no one else can do it for him.

The first four aphorisms of LIGHT ON THE PATH refer entirely to astral development. This development must be accomplished to a certain extent—that is to say, it must be fully entered upon—before the remainder of the book is really intelligible except to the intellect; in fact, before it can be read as a practical, not a metaphysical treatise.

In one of the great mystic Brotherhoods there are four ceremonies that take place early in the year, which practically illustrate and elucidate these aphorisms. They are ceremonies in which only novices take part, for they are simply services of the threshold. But it will show how serious a thing it is to become a disciple, when it is understood that these are all ceremonies of sacrifice. The first one is this of which I have been speaking. The keenest enjoyment, the bitterest pain, the anguish of loss and despair, are brought to bear on the trembling soul, which has not yet found light in the darkness, which is helpless as a blind man is: and until these shocks can be endured without loss of equilibrium the astral senses must remain sealed. This is the merciful law. The " medium," or " spiritualist," who rushes into the psychic world without preparation, is a law-breaker, a breaker of the laws of super-nature. Those who break Nature's laws lose their physical health ; those who break the laws of the inner life lose their psychic health.

" Mediums " become mad, suicides, miserable creatures devoid of moral sense; and often end as unbelievers, doubters even of that which their own eyes have seen. The disciple is compelled to become his own master before he adventures on this perilous path and attempts to face those beings who live and work in the astral world, and whom we call Masters, because of their great knowledge and their ability to control not only themselves but the forces around them.

The condition of the soul when it lives for the life of sensation as distinguished from that of knowledge, is vibratory or oscillating, as distinguished from fixed. That is the nearest literal representation of the fact; but it is only literal to the intellect, not to the intuition. For this part of man's consciousness a different vocabulary is needed. The idea of " fixed " might perhaps be transposed into that of " at home." In sensation no permanent home can be found, because change is the law of this vibratory existence. That fact is the first one which must be learned by the disciple. It is useless to pause and weep for a scene in a kaleidoscope which has passed.

It is a very well known fact, one with which Bulwer Lytton dealt with great power, that an intolerable sadness is the very first experience of the Neophyte in Occultism. A sense of blankness falls upon him which makes the world a waste, and life a vain exertion. This follows his first serious contemplation of the abstract. In gazing, or even in attempting to gaze, on the ineffable mystery of his own higher nature, he himself causes the initial trial to fall on him. The oscillation between pleasure and pain ceases for perhaps an instant of time; but that is enough to have cut him loose from his fast moorings in the world of sensation. He has experienced, however briefly, the greater life; and he goes on with ordinary existence weighted by a sense of unreality, of blank, of horrid negation. This was the nightmare which visited Bulwer Lytton's neophyte in *Zanoni*; and even Zanoni himself, who had learned great truths, and been intrusted with great powers, had not actually passed the threshold where fear and hope, despair and joy, seem at one moment absolute realities, at the next mere forms of fancy.

This initial trial is often brought on us by life itself. For life is, after all, the great teacher. We return to study it, after we have acquired power over it, just as the master in chemistry learns more in the laboratory than his pupil does. There are persons so near the door of knowledge that life itself prepares them for it, and no individual hand has to invoke the hideous guardian of the entrance. These must naturally be keen and powerful organizations, capable of the most vivid pleasure; then pain comes and fills its great duty. The most intense forms of suffering fall on such a nature, till at last it arouses from its stupor of consciousness, and by the force of its internal vitality steps over the threshold into a place of peace. Then the vibration of life loses its power of tyranny. The sensitive nature must suffer still; but the soul has freed itself and stands aloof, guiding the life towards its greatness. Those who are the subjects of Time, and go slowly through all his spaces, live on through a long-drawn series of sensations, and suffer a constant mingling of pleasure and of pain. They do not dare to take the snake of self in a steady grasp and conquer it, so becoming divine; but prefer to go on fretting through divers experiences, suffering blows from the opposing forces.

When one of the subjects of time decides to enter on the path of Occultism, it is this which is his first task. If life has not taught it to him, if he is not strong enough to teach himself, and if he has power enough to demand the help of a Master, then this fearful trial, depicted in *Zanoni*, is put upon him. The oscillation in which he lives is for an instant stilled; and he has to survive the shock of facing what seems to him at first sight as the abyss of nothingness. Not till he has learned to dwell in this abyss, and has found its peace, is it possible for his eyes to have become incapable of tears.

II

BEFORE THE EAR CAN HEAR, IT MUST HAVE LOST ITS SENSITIVENESS

THE first four rules of LIGHT ON THE PATH are undoubtedly, curious though the statement may seem, the most important in the whole book, save one only. Why they are so important is that they contain the vital law, the very creative essence of the astral man. And it is only in the astral (or self-illuminated) consciousness that the rules which follow them have any living meaning. Once attain to the use of the astral senses, and it becomes a matter of course that one commences to use them; and the later rules are but guidance in their use. When I speak like this I mean, naturally, that the first four rules are the ones which are of importance and interest to those who read them in print upon a page. When they are engraved on the man's heart and on his life, unmistakably, then the other rules become not merely interesting or extraordinary, metaphysical statements, but actual facts in life which have to be grasped and experienced.

The four rules stand written in the great chamber of every actual lodge of a living Brotherhood. Whether the man is about to sell his soul to the devil, like Faust; whether he is to be worsted in the battle, like Hamlet; or whether he is to pass on within the precincts; in any case these words are for him. The man can choose between virtue and vice, but not until he is a man; a babe or a wild animal cannot so choose. Thus with the disciple; he must first become a disciple before he can even see the paths to choose between. This effort of creating himself as a disciple, the rebirth, he must do for himself without any teacher. Until the four rules are learned no teacher can be of any use to him; and that is why "the Masters" are referred to in the way they are. No real Masters, whether Adepts in power, in love, or in blackness, can affect a man till these four rules are passed.

Tears, as I have said, may be called the moisture of life. The soul must have laid aside the emotions of humanity, must have secured a balance which cannot be shaken by misfortune, before its eyes can open upon the super-human world.

The voice of the Masters is always in the world; but only those hear it whose ears are no longer receptive of the sounds which affect the personal life. Laughter no longer lightens the heart, anger may no longer enrage it, tender words bring it no balm. For that within, to which the ears are as an outer gateway, is an unshaken place of peace in itself which no person can disturb.

As the eyes are the windows of the soul,
so are the ears its gateways or doors.
Through them comes knowledge of the
confusion of the world. The great ones
who have conquered life, who have become
more than disciples, stand at peace and
undisturbed amid the vibration and kaleido-
scopic movement of humanity. They hold
within themselves a certain knowledge, as
well as a perfect peace; and thus they are
not roused or excited by the partial and
erroneous fragments of information which
are brought to their ears by the changing
voices of those around them. When I
speak of knowledge I mean intuitive knowledge. This certain information can never
be obtained by hard work or by experiment;
for these methods are only applicable to
matter, and matter is in itself a perfectly
uncertain substance, continually affected
by change. The most absolute and universal laws of natural and physical life,
as understood by the scientist, will pass

away when the life of this universe has passed away, and only its soul is left in the silence. What then will be the value of the knowledge of its laws acquired by industry and observation ?

I pray that no reader or critic will imagine that by what I have said I intend to depreciate or disparage acquired knowledge, or the work of scientists. On the contrary, I hold that scientific men are the pioneers of modern thought. The days of literature and of art, when poets and sculptors saw the divine light, and put it into their own great language— these days lie buried in the long past with the ante-Phidian sculptors and the pre-Homeric poets. The Mysteries no longer rule the world of thought and beauty; human life is the governing power, not that which lies beyond it. But the scientific workers are progressing, not so much by their own will as by sheer force of circumstances, towards the far line which divides things interpretable from things uninterpretable. Every fresh discovery drives them a step onward, therefore do I very highly esteem the knowledge obtained by work and experiment.

But intuitive knowledge is an entirely different thing. It is not acquired in any way, but is, so to speak, a faculty of the soul; not the animal soul, that which becomes a ghost after death, when lust or liking or the memory of ill-deeds holds it to the neighbourhood of human beings, but the divine soul which animates all the external forms of the individualized being.

This is, of course, a faculty which indwells in that soul, which is inherent. The would-be disciple has to arouse himself to the consciousness of it by a fierce and resolute and indomitable effort of will. I use the word indomitable for a special reason. Only he who is untamable, who cannot be dominated, who knows he has to play the lord over men, over facts, over all things save his own divinity, can arouse this faculty. "With faith all things are possible." The sceptical laugh at faith, and pride themselves on its absence from their own minds. The truth is that faith is a great engine, an enormous power, which, in fact, can accomplish all things. For it is the covenant or engagement between man's divine part and his lesser self.

The use of this engine is quite necessary in order to obtain intuitive knowledge; for unless a man believes such knowledge exists within himself how can he claim and use it?

Without it he is more helpless than any driftwood or wreckage on the great tides of the ocean. They are cast hither and thither indeed; so may a man be by the chances of fortune. But such adventures are purely external and of very small account. A slave may be dragged through the streets in chains, and yet retain the quiet soul of a philosopher, as was well seen in the person of Epictetus. A man may have every worldly prize in his possession, and stand absolute master of his personal fate, to all appearance, and yet he knows no peace, no certainty, because he is shaken within himself by every tide of thought that he touches on. And these changing tides do not merely sweep the man bodily hither and thither like driftwood on the water; that would be nothing. They enter into the gateways of his soul, and wash over that soul, and make it blind and blank and void of all permanent intelligence, so that passing impressions affect it.

To make my meaning plainer I will use an illustration. Take an author at his writing, a painter at his canvas, a composer listening to the melodies that dawn upon his glad imagination; let any one of these workers pass his daily hours by a wide window looking on a busy street. The power of the animating life blinds sight and hearing alike, and the great traffic of the city goes by like nothing but a passing pageant. But a man whose mind is empty, whose day is objectless, sitting at that same window, notes the passers-by and remembers the faces that chance to please or interest him. So it is with the mind in its relation to eternal truth. If it no longer transmits its fluctuations, its partial knowledge, its unreliable information to the soul; then in the inner place of peace, already found when the first rule has been learned—in that inner place there leaps into flame the light of actual knowledge. Then the ears begin to hear. Very dimly, very faintly at first. And, indeed, so faint and tender are these first indications of the commencement of true, actual life, that they are sometimes pushed aside as mere fancies, mere imaginings. But before these are capable of becoming more than mere imaginings, the abyss of nothingness has to be faced in another form. The utter silence which can only come by closing the ears to all transitory sounds comes as a more appalling horror than even the formless emptiness of space. Our only mental conception of blank space is, I think, when reduced to its barest element of thought, that of black darkness. This is a great physical terror to most persons, and when regarded as an eternal and unchangeable fact, must mean to the mind the idea of annihilation rather than anything else. But it is the obliteration of one sense only; and the sound of a voice may come and bring comfort even in the profoundest darkness. The disciple, having found his way into this blackness, which is the fearful abyss, must then so shut the gates of his soul that no comforter can enter there nor any enemy. And it is in making

this second effort that the fact of pain
and pleasure being but one sensation
becomes recognizable by those who have
before been unable to perceive it. For
when the solitude of silence is reached,
the soul hungers so fiercely and passion-
ately for some sensation on which to rest,
that a painful one would be as keenly
welcomed as a pleasant one. When this
consciousness is reached the courageous
man by seizing and retaining it may destroy the " sensitiveness " at once. When
the ear no longer discriminates between
that which is pleasant or that which is
painful it will no longer be affected by
the voices of others. And then it is safe
and possible to open the doors of the
soul.

" Sight " is the first effort, and the
easiest, because it is accomplished partly
by an intellectual effort. The intellect
can conquer the heart, as is well known
in ordinary life. Therefore this prelimi-

nary step still lies within the dominion of matter. But the second step allows of no such assistance nor of any material aid whatever. Of course, I mean by material aid the action of the brain, or emotions, or human soul. In compelling the ears to listen only to the eternal silence, the being we call man becomes something which is no longer man. A very superficial survey of the thousand and one influences which are brought to bear on us by others will show that this must be so. A disciple will fulfil all the duties of his manhood; but he will fulfil them according to his own sense of right, and not according to that of any person or body of persons. This is a very evident result of following the creed of knowledge instead of any of the blind creeds.

To obtain the pure silence necessary for the disciple, the heart and emotions, the brain and its intellectualisms, have to be put aside. Both are but mechanisms, which will perish with the span of man's life. It is the essence beyond, that which is the motive power, and makes man live, that is now compelled to rouse itself and act. Now is the greatest hour of danger. In the first trial men go mad with fear; of this first trial Bulwer Lytton wrote. No novelist has followed to the second trial, though some of the poets have. Its subtlety and great danger lie in the fact that in the measure of a man's strength is the measure of his chance of passing beyond it or coping with it at all. If he has power enough to awaken that unaccustomed part of himself, the supreme essence, then has he power to lift the Gates of Gold, then he is the true alchemist, in possession of the elixir of life.

It is at this point of experience that the Occultist becomes separated from all other men and enters on to a life which is his own; on to the path of individual accomplishment instead of mere obedience to the genii which rule our earth. This raising of himself into an individual power does in reality identify him with the nobler forces of life, and make him one with them. For they stand beyond the powers of this earth and the laws of this universe. Here lies man's only hope of success in the great effort; to leap right away from his present standpoint to his next, and at once become an intrinsic part of the divine power as he has been an intrinsic part of the intellectual power, of the great nature to which he belongs. He stands always in advance of himself, if such a contradiction can be understood. It is the men who adhere to this position, who believe in their innate power of progress, and that of the whole race, who are the Elder Brothers, the pioneers. Each man has to accomplish the great leap for himself and without aid; yet it is something of a staff to lean on to know that others have gone on that road. It is possible that they have been lost in the abyss; no matter, they have had the courage to enter it. Why I say that it is possible that they have been lost in the abyss is because of this fact, that one who has passed through is unrecognizable until the other and altogether new condition is attained by both. It is unnecessary to enter upon the subject of what that condition is at present. I only say this, that in the early state in which man is entering upon the silence, he loses knowledge of his friends, of his lovers, of all who have been near and dear to him; and also loses sight of his Teachers and of those who have preceded him on his way. I explain this because scarce one passes through without bitter complaint. Could but the mind grasp beforehand that the silence must be complete, surely this complaint need not arise as a hindrance on the Path. Your Teacher or your predecessor may hold your hand in his, and give you the utmost sympathy the human heart is capable of. But when the silence and the darkness come, you lose all knowledge of him; you are alone and he cannot help you, not because his power is gone, but because you have invoked your great enemy.

By your great enemy I mean yourself. If you have the power to face your own soul in the darkness and silence, you will have conquered the physical or animal self which dwells in sensation only.

This statement, I fear, will appear involved, but in reality it is quite simple. Man, when he has reached his fruition, and civilization is at its height, stands between two fires. Could he but claim his great inheritance, the encumbrance of the mere animal life would fall away from him without difficulty. But he does not do this, and so the races of men flower and then droop, and die, and decay off the face of the earth, however splendid the bloom may have been. And it is left to the individual to make this great effort; to refuse to be terrified by his greater nature, to refuse to be drawn back by his lesser or more material self. Every individual who accomplishes this is a redeemer of the race. He may not blazon forth his deeds, he may dwell in secret and silence, but it is a fact that he forms a link between man and his divine part; between the known and the unknown; between the stir of the market-place and the stillness of the snow-capped Himalayas. He has not to go about among men in order to form this link; in the astral he *is* that link, and this fact makes him a being of another order from the rest of mankind. Even so early on the road towards knowledge, when he has but taken the second step, he finds his footing more certain, and becomes conscious that he is a recognized part of a whole.

This is one of the contradictions in life which occur so constantly that they afford fuel to the fiction writer. The Occultist finds them become much more marked as he endeavours to live the life he has chosen. As he retreats within himself and becomes self-dependent, he finds himself more definitely becoming part of a great tide of definite thought and feeling. When he has learned the first lesson, conquered the hunger of the heart, and refused to live on the love of others, he finds himself more capable of inspiring love. As he flings life away, it comes to him in a new form and with a new meaning. The world has always been a place with many contradictions in it to man; when he becomes a disciple he finds life is describable as a series of paradoxes. This is a fact in Nature, and the reason for it is intelligible enough. Man's soul "dwells like a star apart," even that of the vilest among us; while his consciousness is under the law of vibratory and sensuous life. This alone is enough to cause those complications of character which are the material for the novelist; every man is a mystery to friend and enemy alike, and to himself. His motives are often undiscoverable, and he cannot probe to them, or know why he does this or that. The disciple's effort is that of awaking consciousness in this starry part of himself, where his power and divinity lie sleeping. As this consciousness becomes awakened, the contradictions in the man himself become more marked than ever; and so do the paradoxes which he lives through. For, of course, man creates his own life; and "adventures are to the adventurous" is one of those wise proverbs which are drawn from actual fact, and cover the whole area of human experience.

Pressure on the divine part of man reacts upon the animal part. As the

silent soul awakes, it makes the ordinary
life of the man more purposeful, more
vital, more real and responsible. To
keep to the two instances already men-
tioned: the Occultist who has withdrawn
into his own citadel has found his strength;
immediately he becomes aware of the
demands of duty upon him. He does not
obtain his strength by his own right, but
because he is a part of the whole; and
as soon as he is safe from the vibration
of life and can stand unshaken, the outer
world cries out to him to come and labour
in it. So with the heart. When it no
longer wishes to take, it is called upon
to give abundantly. LIGHT ON THE PATH
has been called a book of paradoxes, and
very justly; what else could it be, when
it deals with the actual personal experience of the disciple?

To have acquired the astral senses of
sight and hearing; or, in other words,
to have attained perception and opened

the doors of the soul, are gigantic tasks, and may take the sacrifice of many successive incarnations. And yet, when the will has reached its strength, the whole miracle may be worked in a second of time. Then is the disciple the servant of Time no longer.

These first two steps are negative ; that is to say, they imply retreat from a present condition of things, rather than advance towards another. The next two are active, implying the advance into another state of being.

III

BEFORE THE VOICE CAN SPEAK IN THE PRESENCE OF THE MASTERS

SPEECH is the power of communication; the moment of entrance into active life is marked by its attainment.

And now, before I go any further, let me explain a little the way in which the rules written down in LIGHT ON THE PATH are arranged. The first seven of those which are numbered are sub-divisions of the first two unnumbered rules, those with which I have dealt in the preceding pages. The numbered rules were simply an effort to make the unnumbered ones more intelligible. "Eight" to "fifteen" of these numbered rules belong to this unnumbered rule which is now my text.

As I have said, these rules are written for all disciples, but for none else; they are not of interest to any other persons. Therefore I trust no one else will trouble to read these papers any further. The first two rules include the whole of that part of the effort which necessitates the use of the surgeon's knife. But the disciple is expected to deal with the snake, his lower self, unaided; to suppress his human passions and emotions by the force of his own will. He can only demand assistance of a Master when this is accomplished, or, at all events, partially so. Otherwise the gates and windows of his soul are blurred, and blinded, and darkened, and no knowledge can come to him. I am not, in these papers, purposing to tell a man how to deal with his own soul; I am simply giving, to the disciple, knowledge. That I am not writing, even now, so that all who run may read, is owing to the fact that super-nature prevents this by its own immutable laws.

The four rules which I have written down for those in the West who wish to study them, are, as I have said, written in the ante-chamber of every living Brotherhood; I may add more, in the ante-chamber of every living or dead Brotherhood, or Order yet to be formed. When I speak of a Brotherhood, or an Order, I do not mean an arbitrary constitution made by scholiasts and intellectualists; I mean an actual fact in super-nature, a stage of development towards the absolute God or Good. During this development the disciple encounters harmony, pure knowledge, pure truth, in different degrees, and, as he enters these degrees, he finds himself becoming part of what might be roughly described as a layer of human consciousness. He encounters his equals, men of his own selfless character, and with them his association becomes permanent and indissoluble because founded on a vital likeness of Nature. To them he becomes pledged by such vows as need no utterance or framework in ordinary words. This is one aspect of what I mean by a Brotherhood.

If the first rules are conquered, the disciple finds himself standing at the threshold. Then, if his will be sufficiently resolute his power of speech comes; a twofold power. For, as he advances now, he finds himself entering into a state of blossoming, where every bud that opens throws out its several rays or petals. If he has to exercise his new gift, he must use it in its twofold character. He finds in himself the power to speak in the presence of the Masters; in other words, he has the right to demand contact with the divinest element of that state of consciousness into which he has entered. But he finds himself compelled, by the nature of his position, to act in two ways at the same time. He cannot send his voice up to the heights where sit the gods, till he has penetrated to the deep places where their light shines not at all. He has come within the grip of an iron law. If he demands to become a neophyte, he at once becomes a servant. Yet his service is sublime, if only from the character of those who share it. For the Masters are also servants; they serve, and claim their reward afterwards. Part of their service is to let their knowledge touch him; his first act of service is to give some of that knowledge to those who are not yet fit to stand where he stands. This is no arbitrary decision, made by any Master or Teacher or any such person, however divine. It is a law of that life which the disciple has entered upon.

Therefore was it written in the inner doorway of the Lodges of the old Egyptian Brotherhood, "The labourer is worthy of his hire."

" Ask and ye shall have," sounds like something too easy and simple to be credible. But the disciple cannot " ask " in the mystic sense in which the word is used in this scripture, until he has attained the power of helping others.

Why is this? Has the statement too dogmatic a sound?

Is it too dogmatic to say that a man must have foothold before he can spring? The position is the same. If help is given, if work is done, then there is an actual claim —not what we call a personal claim of payment, but the claim of co-nature. The divine give; they demand that you also shall give before you can be of their kin.

This law is discovered as soon as the disciple endeavours to speak. For speech is a gift which only comes to the disciple of power and knowledge. The spiritualist enters the psychic-astral world, but he does not find there any certain speech, unless he at once claims it and continues to do so. If he is interested in "phenomena," or the mere circumstance and accident of astral life, then he enters no direct ray of thought or purpose; he merely exists and amuses himself in the astral life as he has existed and amused himself in the physical life. Certainly there are one or two simple lessons which the psychic-astral can teach him, just as there are simple lessons which material and intellectual life can teach him. And these lessons have to be learned; the man who proposes to enter upon the life of the disciple without having learned the early and simple lessons must always suffer from his ignorance. They are vital, and have to be studied in a vital manner; experienced through and through, over and over again, so that each part of the nature has been penetrated by them.

To return. In claiming the power of speech, as it is called, the Neophyte cries out to the Great One, Who stands foremost in the ray of knowledge on which he has entered, to give him guidance. When he does this, his voice is hurled back by the power he has approached, and echoes down to the deep recesses of human ignorance. In some confused and blurred manner the news that there is knowledge and a beneficent power which teaches, is carried to as many men as will listen to it. No disciple can cross the threshold without communicating this news, and placing it on record in some fashion or other.

He stands horror-struck at the imperfect and unprepared manner in which he has done this; and then comes the desire to do it well, and with the desire thus to help others comes the power. For it is a pure desire, this which comes upon him; he can gain no credit, no glory, no personal reward by fulfilling it. And therefore he obtains the power to fulfil it.

The history of the whole past, so far as

we can trace it, shows very plainly that there is neither credit, glory, nor reward to be gained by this first task which is given to the Neophyte. Mystics have always been sneered at, and seers disbelieved; those who have had the added power of intellect have left for posterity their written record, which to most men appears unmeaning and visionary, even when the authors have the advantage of speaking from a far-off past. The disciple who undertakes the task, secretly hoping for fame or success, to appear as a teacher and apostle before the world, fails even before his task is attempted, and his hidden hypocrisy poisons his own soul, and the souls of those he teaches. He is secretly worshipping himself, and this idolatrous practice must bring its own reward.

The disciple who has the power of entrance, and is strong enough to pass each barrier, will, when the divine message comes to his spirit, forget himself utterly in the new consciousness which falls on him. If this lofty contact can really rouse him, he becomes as one of the Divine in his desire to give rather than to take, in his wish to help rather than be helped, in his resolution to feed the hungry rather than take manna from heaven himself. His nature is transformed, and the selfishness which prompts men's actions in ordinary life suddenly deserts him.

IV

BEFORE THE VOICE CAN SPEAK IN THE PRE-
SENCE OF THE MASTERS, IT MUST HAVE
LOST THE POWER TO WOUND

THOSE who give a merely passing and
superficial attention to the subject of
Occultism—and their name is legion—
constantly inquire why, if Adepts in life
exist, They do not appear in the world
and show their power. That the chief
body of these Wise Ones should be understood to dwell beyond the fastnesses of
the Himalayas, appears to be a sufficient
proof that They are only figures of straw.
Otherwise why place Them so far off?

Unfortunately, Nature has done this
and not personal choice or arrangement.
There are certain spots on the earth

where the advance of "civilization" is unfelt and the nineteenth-century fever is kept at bay. In these favoured places there is always time, always opportunity, for the realities of life; they are not crowded out by the doings of an inchoate, money-loving, pleasure-seeking society. While there are Adepts upon the earth, the earth must preserve to Them places of seclusion. This is a fact in Nature which is only an external expression of a profound fact in supernature.

The demand of the Neophyte remains unheard until the voice in which it is uttered has lost the power to wound. This is because the divine-astral life is a place in which order reigns, just as it does in natural life. There is, of course, always the centre and the circumference as there is in Nature. Close to the central heart of life, on any plane, there is knowledge; there order reigns completely;

and chaos makes dim and confused the
outer margin of the circle. In fact, life
in every form bears a more or less strong
resemblance to a philosophic school.
There are always the devotees of knowledge who forget their own lives in their
pursuit of it; there are always the flip-
pant crowd who come and go. Of such
Epictetus said that it was as easy to teach
them philosophy as to eat custard with a
fork. The same state exists in the super-
astral life; and the Adept has an even
deeper and more profound seclusion there
in which to dwell. This place of retreat
is so safe, so sheltered, that no sound
which has discord in it can reach His
ears. Why should this be, will be asked
at once, if He be a being of such great
powers as those say who believe in His
existence? The answer seems very ap-
parent. He serves Humanity and identi-
fies Himself with the whole world: He is
ready to make vicarious sacrifice for it at

6

any moment—*by living, not by dying for it.* Why should He not die for it? Because He is part of the great whole, and one of the most valuable parts of it. Because He lives under laws of order which He does not desire to break. His life is not His own, but that of the forces which work behind Him. He is the flower of Humanity, the bloom which contains the Divine Seed. He is, in His own person, a treasure of the universal Nature, which is guarded and made safe in order that the fruition shall be perfected. It is only at definite periods of the world's history that He is allowed to go among the herd of men as their Redeemer. But for those who have the power to separate themselves from this herd, He is always at hand. And for those who are strong enough to conquer the vices of the personal human nature, as set forth in these four rules, He is consciously at hand, easily recognized, ready to answer.

But this conquering of self implies a destruction of qualities which most men regard as not only indestructible but desirable. The "power to wound" includes much that men value, not only in themselves but in others. The instinct of self-defence and of self-preservation is part of it ; the idea that one has any right or rights, either as citizen, or man, or individual, the pleasant consciousness of self-respect and of virtue. These are hard sayings to many, yet they are true. For these words that I am writing now, and those which I have written on this subject, are not in any sense my own. They are drawn from the traditions of the Lodge of the Great Brotherhood, which was once the secret splendour of Egypt. The rules written in its ante-chamber were the same as those now written in the ante-chamber of existing schools. Through all time the wise men have lived apart from the mass. And even when some temporary purpose or object induces one of them to come into the midst of human life, His seclusion and safety are preserved as completely as ever. It is part of His inheritance, part of His position.   He has an actual title to it, and can no more put it aside than the Duke of Westminster can say he does not choose to be the Duke of Westminster.   In the various great cities of the world an Adept lives for a while from time to time, or perhaps only passes through; but all are occasionally aided by the actual power and presence of one of these men.   Here in London, as in Paris and St. Petersburg, there are men high in development.   But They are only known as mystics by those who have the power to recognize; the power given by the conquering of self. Otherwise how could They exist, even for an hour, in such a mental and psychic atmosphere as is created by the confusion and disorder of a city?   Unless protected and made safe, Their own growth would be interfered with, Their work injured. And the Neophyte may meet an Adept in the flesh, may live in the same house with Him, and yet be unable to recognize Him, and unable to make his own voice heard by Him. For no nearness in space, no closeness of relations, no daily intimacy, can do away with the inexorable laws which give the Adept His seclusion. No voice penetrates to His inner hearing till it has become a divine voice, a voice which gives no utterance to the cries of self. Any lesser appeal would be as useless, as much a waste of energy and power, as for mere children who are learning their alphabet to be taught it by a professor of philology. Until a man has become, in heart and spirit, a disciple, he has no existence for those who are Teachers of disciples. And he becomes this by one method only—the surrender of his personal humanity.

For the voice to have lost the power to

wound, a man must have reached that point where he sees himself only as one of the vast multitudes that live; one of the sands washed hither and thither by the sea of vibratory existence. It is said that every grain of sand in the ocean bed does, in its turn, get washed up on to the shore and lie for a moment in the sunshine. So with human beings; they are driven hither and thither by a great force, and each, in his turn, finds the sun-rays on him. When a man is able to regard his own life as part of a whole like this, he will no longer struggle in order to obtain anything for himself. This is the surrender of personal rights. The ordinary man expects, not to take equal fortunes with the rest of the world, but in some points about which he cares, to fare better than the others. The disciple does not expect this. Therefore, though he be like Epictetus, a chained slave, he has no word to say about it. He knows that the wheel of life turns ceaselessly. Burne Jones has shown it, in his marvellous picture; the wheel turns, and on it are bound the rich and the poor, the great and the small; each has his moment of good fortune when the wheel brings him uppermost; the king rises and falls, the poet is *fêted* and forgotten, the slave is happy and afterwards discarded. Each in his turn is crushed as the wheel turns on. The disciple knows that this is so, and though it is his duty to make the utmost of the life that is his, he neither complains of it nor is elated by it, nor does he complain against the better fortune of others. All alike, as he well knows, are but learning a lesson; and he smiles at the socialist and the reformer, who endeavour by sheer force to rearrange circumstances which arise out of the forces of human nature itself. This is but kicking against the pricks, a waste of life and energy.

In realising this a man surrenders his imagined individual rights, of whatever sort. That takes away one keen sting which is common to all ordinary men.

When the disciple has fully recognized that the very thought of individual rights is only the outcome of the venomous quality in himself, that it is the hiss of the snake of self which poisons with its sting his own life and the lives of those about him, then he is ready to take part in a yearly ceremony which is open to all Neophytes who are prepared for it. All weapons of defence and offence are given up; all weapons of mind and heart and brain and spirit. Never again can another man be regarded as a person who can be criticized or condemned; never again can the Neophyte raise his voice in self-defence or excuse. From that ceremony he returns into the world as helpless, as unprotected, as a new-born child. That, indeed, is what he is. He has begun to be born again on to the higher plane of life, that breezy and well-lit plateau whence the eyes see intelligently and regard the world with a new insight.

I have said, a little way back, that after parting with the sense of individual rights, the disciple must part also with the sense of self-respect and of virtue. This may sound a terrible doctrine; yet all Occultists know well that it is not a doctrine, but a fact. He who thinks himself holier than another, he who has any pride in his exemption from vice or folly, he who believes himself wise, or in any way superior to his fellow-men, is incapable of discipleship. A man must become as a little child before he can enter into the kingdom of heaven.

Virtue and wisdom are sublime things; but if they create pride and a consciousness of separateness from the rest of humanity, in the mind of a man, then they are only the snakes of self reappearing in a finer form. At any moment he may put on his grosser shape and sting as fiercely as when he inspired the actions of a murderer who kills for gain or hatred, or a politician who sacrifices the mass for his own or his party's interests.

In fact, to have lost the power to wound implies that the snake is not only scotched, but killed. When it is merely stupefied or lulled to sleep it awakes again, and the disciple uses his knowledge and his power for his own ends, and is a pupil of the many masters of the Black Art, for the road to destruction is very broad and easy, and the way can be found blindfold. That it is the way to destruction is evident, for when a man begins to live for self he narrows his horizon steadily, till at last the fierce driving inwards leaves him but the space of a pin's head to dwell in. We have all seen this phenomenon occur in ordinary life. A man who becomes selfish isolates himself, grows less interesting and less agreeable to others. The sight is an awful one, and people shrink from a very selfish person at last as from a beast of prey. How much more awful is it when it occurs on the more advanced plane of life, with the added powers of knowledge, and through the greater sweep of successive incarnations!

Therefore I say, pause and think well upon the threshold. For if the demand of the Neophyte is made without the complete purification, it will not penetrate the seclusion of the Divine Adept, but will evoke the terrible forces which attend upon the black side of our human nature.

V

BEFORE THE SOUL CAN STAND IN THE
PRESENCE OF THE MASTERS ITS FEET
MUST BE WASHED IN THE BLOOD OF
THE HEART.

THE word Soul, as used here, means the
Divine Soul or " starry Spirit."

" To be able to stand is to have confidence "; and to have confidence means
that the disciple is sure of himself, that
he has surrendered his emotions, his very
self, even his humanity; that he is incapable of fear and unconscious of pain;
that his whole consciousness is centred
in the Divine Life, which is expressed
symbolically by the term, " the Masters ";
that he has neither eyes, nor ears, nor
speech, nor power, save in and for the

Divine Ray on which his highest sense has touched. Then is he fearless, free from suffering, free from anxiety or dismay; his soul stands without shrinking or desire of postponement, in the full blaze of the Divine Light which penetrates through and through his being. Then he has come into his inheritance and can claim his kinship with the Teachers of men; he is upright, he has raised his head, he breathes the same air that They do.

But before it is in any way possible for him to do this, the feet of the soul must be washed in the blood of the heart.

The sacrifice, or surrender, of the heart of man, and his emotions, is the first of the rules; it involves the "attaining of an equilibrium which cannot be shaken by personal emotion." This is done by the stoic philosopher; he, too, stands aside and looks equably upon his own sufferings, as well as on those of others.

In the same way that "tears" in the language of Occultists expresses the soul of emotion, not its material appearance, so blood expresses, not that blood which is an essential of physical life, but the vital creative principle in man's nature, which drives him into human life in order to experience pain and pleasure, joy and sorrow. When he has let the blood flow from the heart, he stands before the Masters as a pure Spirit, which no longer wishes to incarnate for the sake of emotion and experience. Through great cycles of time successive incarnations in gross matter may yet be his lot; but he no longer desires them, the crude wish to live has departed from him. When he takes upon him man's form in the flesh he does it in the pursuit of a divine object, to accomplish the work of "the Masters," and for no other end. He looks neither for pleasure nor pain, asks for no heaven, and fears no hell; yet he has entered upon a great inheritance, which is not so much a compensation for these things surrendered, as a state which simply blots out the memory of them. He lives now not in the world, but with it; his horizon has extended itself to the width of the whole universe.

KARMA

CONSIDER with me that the individual existence is a rope which stretches from the infinite to the infinite, and has no end and no commencement, neither is it capable of being broken. This rope is formed of innumerable fine threads, which, lying closely together, form its thickness. These threads are colourless, are perfect in their qualities of straightness, strength, and levelness. This rope, passing as it does through all places, suffers strange accidents. Very often a thread is caught and becomes attached, or perhaps is only violently pulled away from its even way. Then for a great time it is disordered and it disorders the whole. Sometimes one is stained with dirt or with colour, and not only does the stain run on further than the spot of contact, but it discolours other of the threads. And remember that the threads are living—are like electric wires; more, are like quivering nerves. How far, then, must the stain, the drag awry, be communicated. But eventually the long strands, the living threads which in their unbroken continuity form the individual, pass out of the shadow into the shine. Then the threads are no longer colourless, but golden; once more they lie together, level. Once more harmony is established between them: and from that harmony within the greater harmony is perceived.

This illustration presents but a small portion—a single side of the truth: it is less than a fragment. Yet, dwell on it; by its aid you may be led to perceive more. What it is necessary first to understand is not that the future is arbitrarily formed by any separate acts of the present, but

that the whole of the future is in unbroken
continuity with the present, as the present
is with the past.   On one plane, from one
point of view, the illustration of the rope
is correct.

It is said that a little attention to occultism produces great karmic results.
That is because it is impossible to give any
attention to occultism without making a
definite choice between what are familiarly
called good and evil.   The first step in
occultism brings the student to the tree of
knowledge.   He must pluck and eat; he
must choose.   No longer is he capable of
the indecision of ignorance.   He goes on,
either on the good or on the evil path.
And to step definitely and knowingly even
but one step on either path produces great
karmic results.   The mass of men walk
waveringly, uncertain as to the goal they
aim at; their standard of life is indefinite;
consequently their karma operates in a
confused manner.   But when once the

threshold of knowledge is reached, the confusion begins to lessen, and consequently the karmic results increase enormously, because all are acting in the same direction on all the different planes : for the Occultist cannot be half-hearted, nor can he return when he has passed the threshold. These things are as impossible as that the man should become the child again. The individuality has approached the state to responsibility by reason of growth; it cannot recede from it.

He who would escape from the bondage of Karma must raise his individuality out of the shadow into the shine; must so elevate his existence that these threads do not come in contact with soiling substances, do not become so attached as to be pulled awry. He simply lifts himself out of the region in which Karma operates. He does not leave the existence which he is experiencing because of that. They may be rough and dirty, or full of rich flowers whose pollen stains, and of sweet substances that cling and become attachments—but overhead there is always the free sky. He who desires to be karmaless must look to the air for a home; and after that to the ether. He who desires to form good karma will meet with many confusions, and in the effort to sow rich seed for his own harvesting may plant a thousand weeds, and among them the giant. Desire to sow no seed for your own harvesting: desire only to sow that seed the fruit of which shall feed the world. You are a part of the world; in giving it food you feed yourself. Yet in even this thought there lurks a great danger which starts forward and faces the disciple who has for long thought himself working for good, while in his inmost soul he has perceived only evil; that is, he has thought himself to be intending great benefit to the world while all the time he has unconsciously embraced the thought of Karma, and the great benefit he works for is for himself. A man may refuse to allow himself to think of reward. But in that very refusal is seen the fact that reward is desired. And it is useless for the disciple to strive to learn by means of checking himself. The soul must be unfettered, the desires free. But until they are fixed only on that state wherein there is neither reward nor punishment, good nor evil, it is in vain that he endeavours. He may seem to make great progress, but some day he will come face to face with his own soul, and will recognize that when he came to the tree of knowledge he chose the bitter fruit and not the sweet; and then the veil will fall utterly, and he will give up his freedom and become a slave of desire. Therefore be warned, you who are but turning toward the life of occultism. Learn now that there is no cure for desire, no cure for the love of reward, no cure for the misery of longing, save in the fixing of the sight and hearing upon that which is invisible and soundless. Begin even now to practise it, and so a thousand serpents will be kept from your path. Live in the eternal.

The operation of the actual laws of Karma are not to be studied until the disciple has reached the point at which they no longer affect himself. The initiate has a right to demand the secrets of Nature and to know the rules which govern human life. He obtains this right by having escaped from the limits of Nature and by having freed himself from the rules which govern human life. He has become a recognized portion of the divine element, and is no longer affected by that which is temporary. He then obtains a knowledge of the laws which govern temporary conditions. Therefore you who desire to understand the laws of Karma, attempt first to free yourself from these laws; and this can only be done by fixing your attention on that which is unaffected by those laws.

PRINTED BY NEILL AND CO., LTD., EDINBURGH.

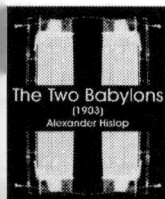

The Two Babylons
Alexander Hislop

QTY

You may be surprised to learn that many traditions of Roman Catholicism in fact don't come from Christ's teachings but from an ancient Babylonian "Mystery" religion that was centered on Nimrod, his wife Semiramis, and a child Tammuz. This book shows how this ancient religion transformed itself as it incorporated Christ into its teachings....

Religion/History   **Pages:358**

ISBN: *1-59462-010-5*   MSRP *$22.95*

The Power Of Concentration
Theron Q. Dumont

It is of the utmost value to learn how to concentrate. To make the greatest success of anything you must be able to concentrate your entire thought upon the idea you are working on. The person that is able to concentrate utilizes all constructive thoughts and shuts out all destructive ones...

Self Help/Inspirational   **Pages:196**

ISBN: *1-59462-141-1*   MSRP *$14.95*

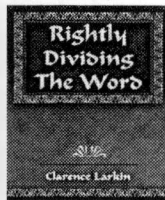

Rightly Dividing The Word
Clarence Larkin

The "Fundamental Doctrines" of the Christian Faith are clearly outlined in numerous books on Theology, but they are not available to the average reader and were mainly written for students. The Author has made it the work of his ministry to preach the "Fundamental Doctrines". To this end he has aimed to express them in the simplest and clearest manner..

Religion   **Pages:352**

ISBN: *1-59462-334-1*   MSRP *$23.45*

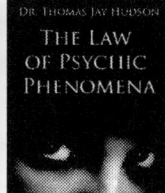

The Law of Psychic Phenomena
Thomson Jay Hudson

"I do not expect this book to stand upon its literary merits; for if it is unsound in principle, felicity of diction cannot save it, and if sound, homeliness of expression cannot destroy it. My primary object in offering it to the public is to assist in bringing Psychology within the domain of the exact sciences. That this has never been accomplished..."

New Age   **Pages:420**

ISBN: *1-59462-124-1*   MSRP *$29.95*

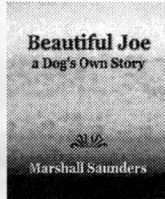

Beautiful Joe
Marshall Saunders

When Marshall visited the Moore family in 1892, she discovered Joe, a dog they had nursed back to health from his previous abusive home to live a happy life. So moved was she, that she wrote this classic masterpiece which won accolades and was recognized as a heartwarming symbol for humane animal treatment...

Fiction   **Pages:256**

ISBN: *1-59462-261-2*   MSRP *$18.45*

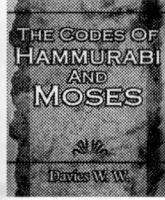

The Codes Of Hammurabi And Moses - W. W. Davies

The discovery of the Hammurabi Code is one of the greatest achievements of archaeology, and is of paramount interest, not only to the student of the Bible, but also to all those interested in ancient history...

Religion   **Pages:132**

ISBN: *1-59462-338-4*   MSRP *$12.95*

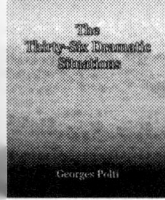

The Thirty-Six Dramatic Situations
Georges Polti

An incredibly useful guide for aspiring authors and playwrights. This volume categorizes every dramatic situation which could occur in a story and describes them in a list of 36 situations. A great aid to help inspire or formalize the creative writing process...

Self Help/Reference   **Pages:204**

ISBN: *1-59462-134-9*   MSRP *$15.95*

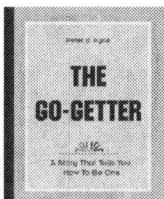

The Go-Getter
Kyne B. Peter

QTY

The Go Getter is the story of William Peck. He was a war veteran and amputee who will not be refused what he wants. Peck not only fights to find employment but continually proves himself more than competent at the many difficult test that are thrown his way in the course of his early days with the Ricks Lumber Company...

Business/Self Help/Inspirational   **Pages:68**

ISBN: *1-59462-186-1*   MSRP *$8.95*

Self Mastery
Emile Coue

Emile Coue came up with novel way to improve the lives of people. He was a pharmacist by trade and often saw ailing people. This lead him to develop autosuggestion, a form of self-hypnosis. At the time his theories weren't popular but over the years evidence is mounting that he was indeed right all along...

New Age/Self Help   **Pages:98**

ISBN: *1-59462-189-6*   MSRP *$7.95*

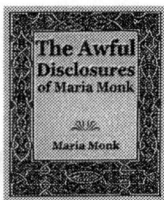

The Awful Disclosures Of Maria Monk

"I cannot banish the scenes and characters of this book from my memory. To me it can never appear like an amusing fable, or lose its interest and importance. The story is one which is continually before me, and must return fresh to my mind with painful emotions as long as I live..."

Religion   **Pages:232**

ISBN: *1-59462-160-8*   MSRP *$17.95*

As a Man Thinketh
James Allen

"This little volume (the result of meditation and experience) is not intended as an exhaustive treatise on the much-written-upon subject of the power of thought. It is suggestive rather than explanatory, its object being to stimulate men and women to the discovery and perception of the truth that by virtue of the thoughts which they choose and encourage..."

Inspirational/Self Help   **Pages:80**

ISBN: *1-59462-231-0*   MSRP *$9.45*

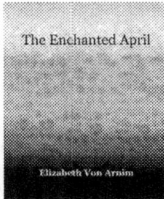

The Enchanted April
Elizabeth Von Arnim

It began in a woman's club in London on a February afternoon, an uncomfortable club, and a miserable afternoon when Mrs. Wilkins, who had come down from Hampstead to shop and had lunched at her club, took up The Times from the table in the smoking-room...

Fiction   **Pages:368**

ISBN: *1-59462-150-0*   MSRP *$23.45*

Holland - The History Of Netherlands
Thomas Colley Grattan

Thomas Grattan was a prestigious writer from Dublin who served as British Consul to the US. Among his works is an authoritative look at the history of Holland. A colorful and interesting look at history....

History/Politics   **Pages:408**

ISBN: *1-59462-137-3*   MSRP *$26.95*

A Concise Dictionary of Middle English
A. L. Mayhew
Walter W. Skeat

The present work is intended to meet, in some measure, the requirements of those who wish to make some study of Middle-English, and who find a difficulty in obtaining such assistance as will enable them to find out the meanings and etymologies of the words most essential to their purpose...

Reference/History   **Pages:332**

ISBN: *1-59462-119-5*   MSRP *$29.95*

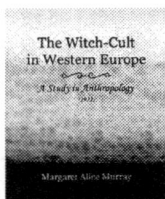

The Witch-Cult in Western Europe
Margaret Murray

QTY

The mass of existing material on this subject is so great that I have not attempted to make a survey of the whole of European "Witchcraft" but have confined myself to an intensive study of the cult in Great Britain. In order, however, to obtain a clearer understanding of the ritual and beliefs I have had recourse to French and Flemish sources...

Occult   Pages:308
ISBN: *1-59462-126-8*   MSRP *$22.45*

The Science Of Psychic Healing
Yogi Ramacharaka

This book is not a book of theories it deals with facts. Its author regards the best of theories as but working hypotheses to be used only until better ones present themselves. The "fact" is the principal thing the essential thing to uncover which the tool, theory, is used...

New Age/Health   Pages:180
ISBN: *1-59462-140-3*   MSRP *$13.95*

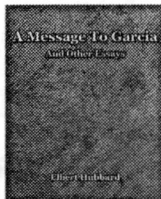

Bible Myths
Thomas Doane

In pursuing the study of the Bible Myths, facts pertaining thereto, in a condensed form, seemed to be greatly needed, and nowhere to be found. Widely scattered through hundreds of ancient and modern volumes, most of the contents of this book may indeed be found; but any previous attempt to trace exclusively the myths and legends...

Religion/History   Pages:644
ISBN: *1-59462-163-2*   MSRP *$38.95*

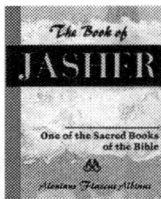

Tertium Organum
P. D. Ouspensky

A truly mind expanding writing that combines science with mysticism with unprecedented elegance. He presents the world we live in as a multi dimensional world and time as a motion through this world. But this isn't a cold and purely analytical explanation but a masterful presentation filled with similes and analogies...

New Age   Pages:356
ISBN: *1-59462-205-1*   MSRP *$23.95*

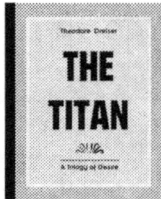

Advance Course in Yogi Philosophy
Yogi Ramacharaka

"The twelve lessons forming this volume were originally issued in the shape of monthly lessons, known as "The Advanced Course in Yogi Philosophy and Oriental Occultism" during a period of twelve months beginning with October, 1904, and ending September, 1905."

Philosophy/Inspirational/Self Help   Pages:340
ISBN: *1-59462-229-9*   MSRP *$22.95*

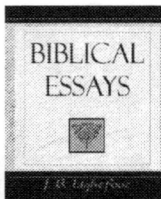

Ambassador Morgenthau's Story
Henry Morgenthau

"By this time the American people have probably become convinced that the Germans deliberately planned the conquest of the world. Yet they hesitate to convict on circumstantial evidence and for this reason all eye witnesses to this, the greatest crime in modern history, should volunteer their testimony..."

History   Pages:472
ISBN: *1-59462-244-2*   MSRP *$29.95*

The Aquarian Gospel of Jesus the Christ
Levi Dowling

A retelling of Jesus' story which tells us what happened during the twenty year gap left by the Bible's New Testament. It tells of his travels to the far-east where he studied with the masters and fought against the rigid caste system. This book has enjoyed a resurgence in modern America and provides spiritual insight with charm. Its influences can be seen throughout the Age of Aquarius.

Religion   Pages:264
ISBN: *1-59462-321-X*   MSRP *$18.95*

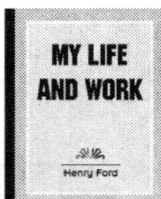

Philosophy Of Natural Therapeutics
Henry Lindlahr

QTY

We invite the earnest cooperation in this great work of all those who have awakened to the necessity for more rational living and for radical reform in healing methods...

Health/Philosophy/Self Help   Pages:552
ISBN: *1-59462-132-2*   MSRP *$34.95*

A Message to Garcia
Elbert Hubbard

This literary trifle, A Message to Garcia, was written one evening after supper, in a single hour. It was on the Twenty-second of February, Eighteen Hundred Ninety-nine, Washington's Birthday, and we were just going to press with the March Philistine...

New Age/Fiction   Pages:92
ISBN: *1-59462-144-6*   MSRP *$9.95*

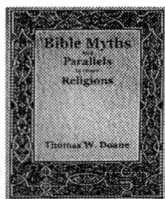

The Book of Jasher
Alcuinus Flaccus Albinus

The Book of Jasher is an historical religious volume that many consider as a missing holy book from the Old Testament. Particularly studied by the Church of Later Day Saints and historians, it covers the history of the world from creation until the period of Judges in Israel. It's authenticity is bolstered due to a reference to the Book of Jasher in the Bible in Joshua 10:13

Religion/History   Pages:276
ISBN: *1-59462-197-7*   MSRP *$18.95*

The Titan
Theodore Dreiser

"When Frank Algernon Cowperwood emerged from the Eastern District Penitentiary, in Philadelphia he realized that the old life he had lived in that city since boyhood was ended. His youth was gone, and with it had been lost the great business prospects of his earlier manhood. He must begin again..."

Fiction   Pages:564
ISBN: *1-59462-220-5*   MSRP *$33.95*

Biblical Essays
J. B. Lightfoot

About one-third of the present volume has already seen the light. The opening essay "On the Internal Evidence for the Authenticity and Genuineness of St John's Gospel" was published in the "Expositor" in the early months of 1890, and has been reprinted since...

Religion/History   Pages:480
ISBN: *1-59462-238-8*   MSRP *$30.95*

The Settlement Cook Book
Simon Kander

A legacy from the civil war, this book is a classic "American charity cookbook," which was used for fundraisers starting in Milwaukee. While it has transformed over the years, this printing provides great recipes from American history. Over two million copies have been sold. This volume contains a rich collection of recipes from noted chefs and hostesses of the turn of the century...

How-to   Pages:472
ISBN: *1-59462-256-6*   MSRP *$29.95*

My Life and Work
Henry Ford

Henry Ford revolutionized the world with his implementation of mass production for the Model T automobile. Gain valuable business insight into his life and work with his own auto-biography... "We have only started on our development of our country we have not as yet, with all our talk of wonderful progress, done more than scratch the surface. The progress has been wonderful enough but..."

Biographies/History/Business   Pages:300
ISBN: *1-59462-198-5*   MSRP *$21.95*

www.bookjungle.com *email: sales@bookjungle.com fax: 630-214-0564 mail: Book Jungle PO Box 2226 Champaign, IL 61825*

QTY

The Rosicrucian Cosmo-Conception Mystic Christianity *by Max Heindel* ISBN: *1-59462-188-8* **$38.95**
The Rosicrucian Cosmo-conception is not dogmatic, neither does it appeal to any other authority than the reason of the student. It is: not controversial, but is: sent forth in the, hope that it may help to clear... New Age/Religion Pages 646

Abandonment To Divine Providence *by Jean-Pierre de Caussade* ISBN: *1-59462-228-0* **$25.95**
"The Rev. Jean Pierre de Caussade was one of the most remarkable spiritual writers of the Society of Jesus in France in the 18th Century. His death took place at Toulouse in 1751. His works have gone through many editions and have been republished... Inspirational/Religion Pages 400

Mental Chemistry *by Charles Haanel* ISBN: *1-59462-192-6* **$23.95**
Mental Chemistry allows the change of material conditions by combining and appropriately utilizing the power of the mind. Much like applied chemistry creates something new and unique out of careful combinations of chemicals the mastery of mental chemistry... New Age Pages 354

The Letters of Robert Browning and Elizabeth Barret Barrett 1845-1846 vol II ISBN: *1-59462-193-4* **$35.95**
by Robert Browning and Elizabeth Barrett Biographies Pages 596

Gleanings In Genesis (volume I) *by Arthur W. Pink* ISBN: *1-59462-130-6* **$27.45**
Appropriately has Genesis been termed "the seed plot of the Bible" for in it we have, in germ form, almost all of the great doctrines which are afterwards fully developed in the books of Scripture which follow... Religion Inspirational Pages 420

The Master Key *by L. W. de Laurence* ISBN: *1-59462-001-6* **$30.95**
In no branch of human knowledge has there been a more lively increase of the spirit of research during the past few years than in the study of Psychology, Concentration and Mental Discipline. The requests for authentic lessons in Thought Control, Mental Discipline and... New Age/Business Pages 422

The Lesser Key Of Solomon Goetia *by L. W. de Laurence* ISBN: *1-59462-092-X* **$9.95**
This translation of the first book of the "Lemegton" which is now for the first time made accessible to students of Talismanic Magic was done, after careful collation and edition, from numerous Ancient Manuscripts in Hebrew, Latin, and French... New Age/Occult Pages 92

Rubaiyat Of Omar Khayyam *by Edward Fitzgerald* ISBN: *1-59462-332-5* **$13.95**
Edward Fitzgerald, whom the world has already learned, in spite of his own efforts to remain within the shadow of anonymity, to look upon as one of the rarest poets of the century, was born at Bredfield, in Suffolk, on the 31st of March, 1809. He was the third son of John Purcell... Music Pages 172

Ancient Law *by Henry Maine* ISBN: *1-59462-128-4* **$29.95**
The chief object of the following pages is to indicate some of the earliest ideas of mankind, as they are reflected in Ancient Law, and to point out the relation of those ideas to modern thought. Religion/History Pages 452

Far-Away Stories *by William J. Locke* ISBN: *1-59462-129-2* **$19.45**
"Good wine needs no bush, but a collection of mixed vintages does. And this book is just such a collection. Some of the stories I do not want to remain buried for ever in the museum files of dead magazine-numbers an author's not unpardonable vanity..." Fiction Pages 272

Life of David Crockett *by David Crockett* ISBN: *1-59462-250-7* **$27.45**
"Colonel David Crockett was one of the most remarkable men of the times in which he lived. Born in humble life, but gifted with a strong will, an indomitable courage, and unremitting perseverance... Biographies/New Age Pages 424

Lip-Reading *by Edward Nitchie* ISBN: *1-59462-206-X* **$25.95**
Edward B. Nitchie, founder of the New York School for the Hard of Hearing, now the Nitchie School of Lip-Reading, Inc, wrote "LIP-READING Principles and Practice". The development and perfecting of this meritorious work on lip-reading was an undertaking... How-to Pages 400

A Handbook of Suggestive Therapeutics, Applied Hypnotism, Psychic Science ISBN: *1-59462-214-0* **$24.95**
by Henry Munro Health New Age Health/Self-help Pages 376

A Doll's House: and Two Other Plays *by Henrik Ibsen* ISBN: *1-59462-112-8* **$19.95**
Henrik Ibsen created this classic when in revolutionary 1848 Rome. Introducing some striking concepts in playwriting for the realist genre, this play has been studied the world over. Fiction/Classics/Plays 308

The Light of Asia *by sir Edwin Arnold* ISBN: *1-59462-204-3* **$13.95**
In this poetic masterpiece, Edwin Arnold describes the life and teachings of Buddha. The man who was to become known as Buddha to the world was born as Prince Gautama of India but he rejected the worldly riches and abandoned the reigns of power when... Religion/History/Biographies Pages 170

The Complete Works of Guy de Maupassant *by Guy de Maupassant* ISBN: *1-59462-157-8* **$16.95**
"For days and days, nights and nights, I had dreamed of that first kiss which was to consecrate our engagement, and I knew not on what spot I should put my lips..." Fiction/Classics Pages 240

The Art of Cross-Examination *by Francis L. Wellman* ISBN: *1-59462-309-0* **$26.95**
Written by a renowned trial lawyer, Wellman imparts his experience and uses case studies to explain how to use psychology to extract desired information through questioning. How-to Science/Reference Pages 408

Answered or Unanswered? *by Louisa Vaughan* ISBN: *1-59462-248-5* **$10.95**
Miracles of Faith in China Religion Pages 112

The Edinburgh Lectures on Mental Science (1909) *by Thomas* ISBN: *1-59462-008-3* **$11.95**
This book contains the substance of a course of lectures recently given by the writer in the Queen Street Hall, Edinburgh. Its purpose is to indicate the Natural Principles governing the relation between Mental Action and Material Conditions... New Age Psychology Pages 148

Ayesha *by H. Rider Haggard* ISBN: *1-59462-301-5* **$24.95**
Verily and indeed it is the unexpected that happens! Probably if there was one person upon the earth from whom the Editor of this, and of a certain previous history, did not expect to hear again... Classics Pages 380

Ayala's Angel *by Anthony Trollope* ISBN: *1-59462-352-X* **$29.95**
The two girls were both pretty, but Lucy who was twenty-one who supposed to be simple and comparatively unattractive, whereas Ayala was credited, as her Bombwhat romantic name might show, with poetic charm and a taste for romance. Ayala when her father died was nineteen... Fiction Pages 484

The American Commonwealth *by James Bryce* ISBN: *1-59462-286-8* **$34.45**
An interpretation of American democratic political theory. It examines political mechanics and society from the perspective of Scotsman James Bryce Politics Pages 572

Stories of the Pilgrims *by Margaret P. Pumphrey* ISBN: *1-59462-116-0* **$17.95**
This book explores pilgrims religious oppression in England as well as their escape to Holland and eventual crossing to America on the Mayflower, and their early days in New England... History Pages 268

QTY

The Fasting Cure *by Sinclair Upton* ISBN: *1-59462-222-1* **$13.95**
In the Cosmopolitan Magazine for May, 1910, and in the Contemporary Review (London) for April, 1910, I published an article dealing with my experiences in fasting. I have written a great many magazine articles, but never one which attracted so much attention... New Age/Self Help/Health Pages 164

Hebrew Astrology *by Sepharial* ISBN: *1-59462-308-2* **$13.45**
In these days of advanced thinking it is a matter of common observation that we have left many of the old landmarks behind and that we are now pressing forward to greater heights and to a wider horizon than that which represented the mind-content of our progenitors... Astrology Pages 144

Thought Vibration or The Law of Attraction in the Thought World ISBN: *1-59462-127-6* **$12.95**
by William Walker Atkinson Psychology/Religion Pages 144

Optimism *by Helen Keller* ISBN: *1-59462-108-X* **$15.95**
Helen Keller was blind, deaf, and mute since 19 months old, yet famously learned how to overcome these handicaps, communicate with the world, and spread her lectures promoting optimism. An inspiring read for everyone... Biographies/Inspirational Pages 84

Sara Crewe *by Frances Burnett* ISBN: *1-59462-360-0* **$9.45**
In the first place, Miss Minchin lived in London. Her home was a large, dull, tall one, in a large, dull square, where all the houses were alike, and all the sparrows were alike, and where all the door-knockers made the same heavy sound... Childrens/Classic Pages 88

The Autobiography of Benjamin Franklin *by Benjamin Franklin* ISBN: *1-59462-135-7* **$24.95**
The Autobiography of Benjamin Franklin has probably been more extensively read than any other American historical work, and no other book of its kind has had such ups and downs of fortune. Franklin lived for many years in England, where he was agent... Biographies/History Pages 332

Name	
Email	
Telephone	
Address	
City, State ZIP	

☐ **Credit Card**   ☐ **Check / Money Order**

Credit Card Number	
Expiration Date	
Signature	

Please Mail to: Book Jungle
PO Box 2226
Champaign, IL 61825
or Fax to: 630-214-0564

ORDERING INFORMATION

web: *www.bookjungle.com*
email: *sales@bookjungle.com*
fax: *630-214-0564*
mail: *Book Jungle PO Box 2226 Champaign, IL 61825*
or PayPal *to sales@bookjungle.com*

Please contact us for bulk discounts

DIRECT-ORDER TERMS

20% Discount if You Order Two or More Books
Free Domestic Shipping!
Accepted: Master Card, Visa, Discover, American Express